Life Matches: Fire Up Your Life!

By Andrew Dix

Life Matches: Fire Up Your Life!

ISBN 978-1-60910-257-9

Printed in the United States of America.

BookLocker.com, Inc.
2010

Grateful acknowledgment is made to the publisher for permission to reprint the following work: Rath, T., *StrengthsFinder 2.0*, published by Gallup Press, New York, 2007.

Acknowledgements

I once heard a story about what is called the "sin of the desert." The main premise of this story is that it is a mortal sin for someone who knows the location of water in the desert to not share that location with fellow desert travelers. I thank the many teachers, co-workers, friends and family who have generously shared so much of their life's knowledge with me, so that I can pass along its location to you with this book. They will never be accused of committing the sin of the desert.

I thank Rev. Rodney Frieden, Ray Hilbert, Ken Gandy, Esq., Tom Balcerzak, Esq., Ed Hawes, the members of the TGIF Men's Group, Phil Paligraf, Roland Trombley and the many members of my work family. I could never have completed this book without their encouragement and support.

Special thanks to Julie Rollins for donating her time and grammatical expertise to edit and improve this book.

The illustrations which grace this book are thanks to my wife's best friend, the incredibly talented Beth Hilbert, who donated her gifts and also graciously allows her husband, Ray, to pal around with me and laugh like teenagers.

I am most grateful for the love, understanding and support of my wife, Kathy, and my two beautiful daughters, Samantha and Sarah. Don't worry, Daddy will be done soon and we can all go for a bike ride!

I believe that this story was given to me by God to share with you. It has been my privilege to do so. My hope and prayer is that everyone who reads this book may enjoy the warm satisfaction of living a strengths-based life in service to the giver of all gifts.

Thank you.

A very fired up!

Andy

(March 2010, Indianapolis, Indiana)

Author's Note

All of the author's profits from this book will be donated to Children and Adults with Attention Deficit/Hyperactivity Disorder (CHADD), a national non-profit organization working to improve the lives of affected people through education, advocacy and support. To learn more about CHADD, visit the website at http://www.chadd.org.

People who have AD/HD have amazing strengths. Many of the professionals and caring CHADD members dedicate their lives to help those with AD/HD find ways to fire up their lives!

Table of Contents

Preface

I am a perpetual self-helper. I find I am constantly looking for ways to improve my life and learn ideas that can help me move up Abraham Maslow's hierarchy of needs to the pinnacle of self-actualization. Unfortunately, I have not found much of the life tips and techniques lasting, and I have followed the bouncing improvement ball from topic to topic. When whatever I was trying to improve grew to be too difficult a task, or just boring, I moved on to the next area of possible improvement. So many weaknesses, so little time might have been my life motto. Then I came across a book published by the Gallup Organization titled, *StrengthsFinder 2.0*[1], written by Tom Rath and its online profile. The strengths-based concepts for lasting personal growth sparked my imagination and resulted in the book you are now reading.

Life Matches is a way of thinking about your God-given strengths and talents. You can make your own book of Life Matches to serve as a physical reminder that you can carry with you to remember to focus on your strengths so that you can become a powerful light in our world.

No one else has been or will ever again be created with exactly the same mixture of strengths that you have been given. I believe it is your personal quest in this journey called life to learn all that you can and to make the most out of what you have been given. I personally believe that you will find the most satisfaction through using your strengths in service to others. Choosing to be selfish or solely ego-

---

[1]Rath, T., *StrengthsFinder 2.0*, published by Gallup Press, New York, 2007.

driven in using your strengths may result in worldly success that you ultimately will find meaningless. My wish for you is to seek and to experience the joy of living a satisfied life through knowing that you have lived your life on purpose and have achieved your fullest potential through selfless service to mankind and our world.

Please understand my underlying perspective and bias that I bring to this book. I am a disciple of Jesus Christ. I believe that we are each created by a loving God who uniquely crafted a specific set of personal gifts and talents into each of our beings. He challenges us to surrender our gifts to use as He sees fit to glorify His name. Discipleship means being a student of a master, or as I prefer to think of it, discipleship means being a lifelong trainee of Christ. This way, when I learn life lessons, typically by making monumental mistakes, I know it is okay, because I am only a trainee in this life and if I ask sincerely, I am forgiven and can try again. Fortunately, unlike me, God doesn't make mistakes. You are the way you are for His reasons. It is up to you to ask Him to reveal your ultimate life's purpose or reason for being. Don't worry. He will.

As a start, pray the following prayer:

"God, thank you for creating me with so many personal gifts and talents and for giving me my entire lifetime to learn how to best use them. Help me to learn which ones you will have me use and teach me how you would have me use them in ways that bring light through service to others in this world. Please show me your purpose that you have created uniquely for me and give me the courage, faith and trust that through you all things are possible. Keep my ego and pride in check through both successes and failures. Please allow me

to savor the satisfaction of a well-lived life that was lived purposefully in service to your glory. In Christ's name I pray. Amen."

You will definitely know when you are on the right track. Your life will be fired up as you live your life on purpose, using your strengths in the way that you were exclusively designed to do. Read on and see if together we can spark a passionate life full of successful satisfaction.

2 Timothy 1:6

Chapter 1: A Sign of Weakness

7:03 p.m. is displayed in the lower right hand corner of the computer screen of Tim Davis, director of sales for MegaAds Indiana. I really need to review these sales figures before tomorrow's conference call, but I also have to get a handle on how many commercials we have left to sell in next week's NFL football game, Tim thought to himself as he set his glasses on his desk and rubbed his forehead. What did I name that inventory tracking spreadsheet? he asked himself out loud since everyone else had left the advertising sales office for home hours earlier. Exhausted, Tim thought, Am I done yet? Feeling exhausted was almost a normal feeling for Tim.

Tim's desk phone rang and Joanne, his wife of 24 years coolly stated, "Hi, your dinner is waiting for you in the microwave and will stay somewhat edible if you can peel yourself away from your office long enough to come home to eat it before midnight."

"I'm sorry honey, but I have a couple of things to wrap up and then I'll be out of here, I promise," replied Tim. He waited for Joanne's usual frustrated tirade, but was surprised with a curt okay from her as the line went dead. "That can't be good," Tim sighed as he hung up the receiver. "When was the last time we all sat down for a family dinner? One, maybe two weeks? I hope it hasn't been longer, since I don't exactly know when we last all ate together at home."

An e-mail summary popped up on Tim's screen notifying him that he had received a message from Ray Sikes, the advertising manager for one of MegaAd's largest clients. The subject said it all--"WRONG COMMERCIAL RUNNING!!! CANCEL REST OF YEAR!!!!"-- then disappeared from view. Tim's shirt collar button and necktie, which were unbuttoned and somewhat loose, suddenly felt too tight and he unconsciously tried to make them looser around his neck. His heart pounded at the thought of losing well over $1 million in advertising revenue for the rest of this year. A wave of nausea swept over Tim. He felt his fingers oddly tingle as a cold sweat broke out over his body. Tim also quickly realized that he was having trouble catching his breath. Am I having a heart attack? a now panic-stricken Tim thought.

Dizzy and feeling foolish while doing it, he dialed 911 from his cellular telephone. While he was having his brief exchange with the emergency operator, he turned off his computer, turned off his office lights, locked his door and went to the front entrance and waited for the paramedics to arrive from the fire station only 300 yards up the street from his office building. Tim watched as the red flashing lights reflected off nearby buildings as the ambulance pulled out of the station and onto the street. Its siren wailed only two times before the ambulance turned into the parking lot and pulled up to Tim, who was sitting on the curb.

The emergency medical technicians were professional and efficient in their task of assessing Tim's physical condition and after completing their preliminary treatments, they transported him to the nearby hospital.

Tim felt more like a detached observer than the patient as the emergency room staff attached various monitors, checked his pulse and blood pressure, drew blood, and inserted a stent into a vein in his arm.

The emergency room physician was friendly and a few years younger than Tim. He reviewed Tim's initial results and told him what to expect in the next couple of hours. His plan was to continue to monitor his condition and run further tests. Assuming that nothing abnormal was uncovered, Tim would be given a stress test on a treadmill and would be administered an ultrasound of his heart.

The ER doctor finally gave Tim what he called an antacid cocktail to see if it eased his chest pains. Tim drank the thick substance and within minutes the burning in his chest stopped. According to the doctor, this was a very good sign that Tim's chest pain was most likely the result of painful heartburn and not caused by a heart attack. Tim felt a wave of relief on hearing the news and began to calm down.

Surrounded by an opaque curtain, alone in his hospital bed, Tim listened to the busy activities and suffering which surrounded him in the emergency room. With nothing else to hold his attention, he watched the colorful heart monitor as his heartbeats were converted into a moving graph with each peak further proof that he was alive. The automatic blood pressure cuff would constrict to the point of being painful as it filled with air on his left bicep. Tim tried to relax by taking deep breaths to see if he could will his blood pressure reading lower. He had nothing else to do but breathe and wait for a verdict from his doctor. His mind plagued him with a recurrent waking nightmare of a death sentence.

A weary and grateful-to-be-alive Tim was finally wheeled into the hospital lobby's entranceway from the emergency room in a wheelchair to await a taxi to take him to his car at his office. It was well past midnight and he was both relieved and embarrassed to have been diagnosed with heartburn and a panic attack instead of a heart attack. Oh, Joanne is going to really love this, thought Tim. She has been nagging me about taking some time off and to not work so many hours. Even if I don't really like what I do anymore, I feel responsible for doing a good job and that means forcing me to put in the hours to get it all done.

Five voice mail messages showed on his Blackberry, which had sat unattended for the first time in months while he was poked and prodded by the cardiac care ER staff. Tim also saw the red LED flashing, indicating a new e-mail message sent from Joanne over an hour ago, which read, "Where r u?"

Tim hated himself for running in fear to the hospital thinking this was just another sure sign of weakness on his part. He felt like he had been burning the candle at both ends and the middle for months now. In a moment of truth, he realized he was more "working" his life than really "living" it. He felt trapped in a cage of his own making and was unable to see a way out. Tim rationalized, I guess that's why they pay me the big bucks. His thought gave him little consolation and his mood sank into the darkness.

A yellow taxi pulled into the hospital patient pick-up area and stopped in front of a brooding Tim.

"You need a taxi, sir?" asked the cab driver in a thick foreign accent, the origin of which Tim did not recognize. "Where to, sir?" he asked.

"Yes, thanks, 7444 Shadeland," replied Tim as he settled into the taxi's back seat, very grateful to be out of the hospital with little more than a standard warning to take it a little easier, start exercising and lose some weight, as advised by his new cardiologist.

Alone in his car in the office parking lot, Tim detected from Joanne's worried tone in the voice mail messages she left that she too had a long night.

"Sorry, JoJo, but I didn't want to worry you and the girls when I knew it was going to turn out to be nothing and surely enough, it did," quickly explained Tim via his Blackberry phone, trying to sound upbeat and positive.

"I'm thankful you're okay, but you have no idea how scared and upset we've been," said Joanne. "How could you be so selfish as to not even call us from the hospital?" Joanne sounded a turbulent blend of frustration, anger, fear and as if she was fighting back tears. Finally giving into a sob, she burst out, "Tim, what if you died and we didn't even know it?"

Tim did not really hear the rest of the conversation. Nor did he remember the rest of the drive to his luxurious, executive home in a distant suburb of Indianapolis. "What if you died?" kept ringing again and again in his head, right through the worried but relieved hug from Joanne and throughout the all too short, restless night. Tim awoke with the nagging question of his death still on the top in his mind. He was the first person in the office. His hand was frozen on his computer mouse as he tried to muster the courage to read the ominous Sikes e-mail.

Sometimes lately it feels like this mouse weighs a ton. I know I have to do this, but I really do not want to do it. He indulged in a brief fantasy of deleting the message instead of opening it. What a way to start the day. Maybe this isn't worth the big bucks they pay me to do it, silently groused Tim as he clicked on the message to open the e-mail from Mr. Sikes and he began to read....

Still somewhat physically exhausted and mentally down from last night's excitement, Tim set his glasses on his desk and leaned forward with his hands over his eyes to shut out the reality of the words on his computer screen and to think what he should do about Sikes. He was unable to focus on the Sikes issue because his mind persistently questioned what he should do about his life. Also fighting for his attention was the now ever-present echo which seemed to grow louder by the minute of Joanne's voice asking him "What if you died?" This was certainly not a good morning and the afternoon did not hold the prospect of much improvement.

Paul Andrews, the newly promoted director of workplace learning and development, faked a cough as he helped himself to a ladle full of peanut M&Ms from Tim's desk candy jar. He did not want to startle Tim, who appeared either deep in thought, praying or maybe even asleep.

Without moving, Tim cautioned, "Do not even ask how it's going. I guarantee that you won't like my answer."

"Wow, sounds rough. Do you want to talk about it?" asked Paul as he popped half of a handful of M&Ms into his mouth.

A part of Tim wanted desperately to talk about his situation and so-called life, but he did not want to appear weak to anyone, especially to Paul because he had held Tim's job prior to his promotion.

Masking his personal pain behind his best poker face, Tim unconvincingly replied, "Not really."

Suspecting the gravity of the situation, Paul told Tim that he understood and would be willing to listen or try to help, if Tim wanted him to do so. "Aside from the need for a free snack, the main reason I stopped by was to see if you might take some time to review a short learning session I've been working on for the upcoming managers' summit meeting?" asked Paul. He suggested that he and Tim get together next week for lunch and allow Paul to present the lesson to Tim.

"I'll even buy lunch to get your undivided attention and input!" joked Paul. Reluctantly, Tim agreed to lunch at 11:00 a.m. on Monday.

Chapter 2: Home Sweet Home

Tim's day dragged on and down from there. Thank God it's Friday, thought Tim more than once throughout the day. At 7:10 p.m., Tim left for home and a quiet dinner with JoJo and his two young daughters, Savannah, age 11 and eight-year-old Stephanie.

Tim was right about the quiet part, as he was served a distant-feeling silence by the ladies of the house. Even Walter, his loyal basset hound, seemed to be too comfortable in his dog bed to be bothered with greeting him.

Feeling the mounting silent resentment and rejection, Tim inwardly lamented. My first night home in two or three weeks for dinner and this is the kind of treatment I get? I guess the breadwinner gets to eat his bread buttered with the silent treatment tonight. A very tired, lonely and somewhat overwhelmed Tim ruminated throughout the rest of their mealtime as he pushed his food around on his plate due to a sudden lack of appetite.

After dinner, Tim settled into his favorite recliner with an after dinner cocktail in hand to flip channels on his wall-mounted large-screen television. From the corner of his eye he saw Savannah sitting at his home office desk at the computer, squirming. Savannah was diagnosed a year ago by a psychologist as having Attention Deficit Hyperactivity Disorder (AD/HD) and struggled to pay attention in school and to focus on her homework, among other social and family issues that are caused by her symptoms.

Savannah had shown great improvements of late, thanks to a token reward system Joanne had set up to reward good behaviors. A large checklist of daily tasks, such as putting clean dishes into the cabinets and making her bed, hung on the refrigerator. It also listed the corresponding number of poker chips that Savannah would receive for successfully completing the task. The poker chips could be redeemed like money to purchase small reward items which she had previously selected and Joanne had purchased and displayed on top of the refrigerator like a small success store. This reward system, combined with the correct dosage of stimulant medication and a lot of behavioral coaching and practice, allowed Savannah to manage her disability relatively well and to earn B and C grades at school.

Savannah named her medication "smart pills" since it allowed her brain to process information much more effectively and gave her the mental ability to focus on her school work. Behavioral and judgment problems occurred as the time release medication was usually out of her system by the end of the school day. Without the help from her medication, her symptoms made working on homework a real challenge on a good day and an outright battle on a bad day. On most school days Tim was at work, so homework hassles were left to Joanne.

A wave of guilt washed over Tim as he watched Savannah grow frustrated and agitated at the computer. Savannah's face flashed various colors as the screen's image reflected off her glasses and cheeks. "Mom! I can't get to a picture of the Amazon rain forest because of this stupid blocking software you put on my account! I NEED YOUR HELP!" Savannah shrieked as her patience ran out and frustration seized control of her mind.

Joanne, who was still cleaning the dinner dishes while listening to Stephanie read a storybook out loud to her, sarcastically shouted down the hallway, "Can the other parent in the house please see if he can help his daughter with her homework for once?" The ego-bruising verbal blow landed as intended and a reluctant Tim turned off the television and walked down the short hallway to see if he could fix Savannah's problem.

Without the help of her medication, Savannah's frustration quickly evolved into anger as an emotional seizure took control of her behavior. While in this highly agitated state, Savannah's thoughts instantly turned into actions that were beyond her direct control. These emotional outbursts often lasted for a few minutes with some tantrums lasting much longer.

The hardest part of Savannah's disability for Tim, who found trying to work with Savannah so frustrating, was that she looked like any other "normal" 11-year-old, but she acted out like a child of seven or eight. Without medication, she could be terribly hateful and disrespectful to everyone in the family. Tim found this especially challenging as he was frustrated by his lack of control over the situation and worse yet, his ever-present feelings of failure as a parent whenever he dealt with Savannah's AD/HD episodes.

Even when he took the time to make an effort to help her, it usually ended in a bitter argument. Failure was a feeling Tim hated and tried to avoid, even if it meant that he avoided helping his family by leaving the heavy-duty, emotionally-hazardous parenting to a resentful and overburdened Joanne.

Being the boss meant that people at work were generally expected to listen, respect and do as Tim directed with little argument. This gave Tim a sense of being in control of the situation. Feeling in control was a feeling he enjoyed. At home, Tim felt inadequate and often out of control and not respected. In brief moments of self-honesty, he felt like he worked harder at home putting out fires and solving other peoples' problems than he did at work. He certainly believed he was more effective as a leader at work than he had been in the role of husband and father at home.

Tim reflexively dodged the wireless mouse as it whizzed past his head and out the home office doorway. Savannah, who had been blessed with a strong throwing arm, probably had not intended to hit Tim with the mouse. He had just happened to be at the wrong place at the wrong time.

A wild-eyed Savannah swiveled the chair to face her somewhat bewildered father. With angry tears visibly formed behind her glasses, she yelled in rapid fire, "I hate this computer! Why did Mom and you have to block everything on the Internet? I can't get anything done for my stupid homework and it's all your fault!"

Instinctively, Tim was at once angry to have been almost hit by a flying computer mouse and to have been under assault by Savannah's vicious verbal attack. Both Tim's jaw and hands clenched as he tried to maintain control of his rising emotions.

Tim flashed to what Savannah's therapist had told him: she had a disability just like a child in a wheelchair and no reasonable person would get mad at a wheelchair-bound child for not standing up and running a race. A hard part for AD/HD children was their disability's symptoms were often just as real and as severe, but there was not a wheelchair to remind others of their disability.

Tim forced himself to take a deep breath and to let it out before he jumped into battle with Savannah. But before he could get a word out, he was pushed aside by Joanne, who had rushed in after hearing the mouse bounce down the hardwood hallway floor.

"Tim, just let me handle this," admonished Joanne. "You should just go watch TV."

As Joanne began to engage Savannah and bring her back into emotional control, Tim dejectedly left the room and returned to the solitude of the living room. Toasting yet another fatherly failure, Tim raised his glass to Walter the basset hound and stated "Home sweet home" before he swallowed hard a large swig of his cocktail and changed the channel on the television.

Saturday was typical for Tim. After a fitful night, he was awake at his usual 5:00 a.m. and finished his second cup of coffee from his leather recliner in the grey-blue light of the pre-dawn. This was usually Tim's personal quiet time. Under the side table next to Tim's chair rested a Bible and daily devotional that needed a good dusting. Kind of like my faith, Tim thought as he brushed his hand over the cover of the devotional. Maybe I'll read today's lesson before bed tonight, he thought as he picked up his Blackberry to check the news headlines.

If a story bleeds it leads was certainly true this morning. Tim shuddered with a cold chill as he viewed an angelic-looking picture of an 11-year-old girl from Maine. Her body was found dead in a wooded area, less than two miles from her home and nine days after her abduction. The photo had obviously been taken at Christmas due to the lighted tree in the background.

The girl's sparkling eyes in the small photo on Tim's Blackberry screen overwhelmed his emotional defenses and Tim Davis, director of sales, wept. Fairness and justice were core beliefs of his and this tragedy offended both. What if I had died and couldn't protect my family from this kind of human evil, sobbed Tim quietly to himself.

The rest of the day Tim locked himself away in his study to work on a monthly report which was due to his boss on Monday. He only took breaks for a quick lunch and dinner. Joanne and the girls had not seemed to notice or care about Tim's self-imposed absence.

Joanne was surprised to see Tim showered, shaved and dressed for church on Sunday morning. It had been months since the family had attended a worship service together. She decided not to ask about Tim's motivation, but rather she just thanked God that he was joining his family.

The church sanctuary was cozy and a little warm. After only a few minutes of the minister's sermon, Tim drifted and then dozed. The vibrations of an incoming e-mail message from his Blackberry startled him as he woke to hear his minister reading from the book of Romans, "We have different gifts, according to the grace given us."

Chapter 3: A Gift You Can Use

Paul was pleased to see that Tim not only had arrived, but was on time and seemed to be in a reasonable mood for their Monday lunch meeting. Shaking Tim's hand, Paul said, "I won't ask you how it's going. Instead, I'll simply say thanks for coming! I'm glad to see you and can't wait to get your take on my session for the managers' summit meeting."

"I'll need to make this quick, because I have a conference call at one o'clock."

Paul nodded. "Not a problem. This shouldn't take long as it's really more of a story or maybe even a parable than a presentation."

Tim and Paul ordered their food and drinks and after their server left their table, Paul said to Tim, "I have a free gift for you. It's a gift you can use, if you choose to accept it."

Tim looked somewhat apprehensively across the table at Paul and said a long, cautious, "Okay…."

Paul reached into his shirt pocket and tossed across the table to Tim a white book of cardboard matches with red words printed on it.

Somewhat surprised, Tim looked at the book of matches and with a touch of sarcasm said, "Ah, thanks Paul, this is just what I needed. I've been considering some life changes lately. Maybe taking up smoking is the answer or better yet, perhaps a little arson could put an end to my overflowing inbasket and to-do list."

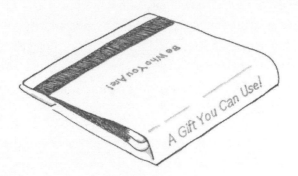

Paul smiled, "You've just discovered two of the main points of my gift. As you can see, printed on the spine of the matchbook are the words, 'A Gift You Can Use.' So, my first point is that this book of matches is a gift you can use however you choose. You can even choose to throw them away or to never use them. The choice is totally yours."

"Profound," Tim said with an even larger hint of sarcasm than before as he glanced around the room for the server.

Undaunted by Tim's sarcasm, Paul continued, "Point number two is that you have done nothing to deserve or earn this gift. It was freely given to you. But as with any gift, you must choose to accept it." Paul paused for dramatic effect and then looked Tim squarely in the eyes and asked him, "Do you accept this free gift?"

Tim made a short, outward sniff of his nose that turned into a slight smile, "Of course Paul, how could I ever refuse such a wonderful and useful gift?"

"You'd be surprised at how many people refuse the gifts they've been given, or even worse yet, accept the gift and then fail to ever use it. So let me begin at the beginning. I call the gift you've just received, 'Life Matches.' It's a physical reminder of the material I've been preparing for the managers' summit meeting on strengths-based leadership.

"The concept was formed from the research of a worldwide survey of peoples' areas of personal strengths and weaknesses, conducted by the Gallup Organization and written about in a book called *StrengthsFinder 2.0* by Tom Rath. Gallup's scientists, led by Dr. Donald O. Clifton in 1998, developed an assessment tool to allow a person to analyze 34 different areas of his or her life and discover what gifts and talents he or she might have. Once we know what our areas of strength and talents are, then the question becomes how do we put our strengths to use?"

The server, upon seeing the book of matches in Tim's hands as he served lunch, cautioned that it was a smoke-free restaurant. To which Tim replied, "I think the only smoke is coming from the guy across the table from me and is directed up my dress!" Politely smiling, the server left having issued his warning.

Paul began again, "This Gallup study has been conducted over the past 40 years and I can assure you that it is quite comprehensive, valid and reliable. Let me go over some of the highlights from the study that I was hoping to touch on during the managers' summit meeting.

"First, out of 10 million people Gallup surveyed, only about 30 percent think they have the opportunity to do what they do best

16

every day at their jobs. That means around 70 percent of people don't have the opportunity to do what they do best every day on their jobs."

Tim nodded empathetically.

"Secondly, a survey showed that of the people who said they don't get to do what they do best or exercise their strengths on the job, every one of those people were not 'emotionally engaged' in their work.

"And thirdly, people who do get to work daily using their strengths report 600 percent more on-the-job engagement and 300 percent agreement with having an excellent quality of life in general."

"So basically," Tim interrupted Paul, "what you're telling me is that if you get to do what you like to do, and what you're good at doing daily on your job, you will like your job and life more? What a news flash!" exclaimed Tim with a fresh dose of sarcasm. "So, where and how, do your little matches come into play?"

"My Life Matches," Paul countered, "come into play to reinforce the point of remembering to focus on your natural, God-given strengths, gifts and talents instead of wasting energy, time and efforts in a losing battle to improve your weaknesses. Let me demonstrate my point with the help of your new 'Life Matches' matchbook."

Chapter 4: A "Sign" of Your Strengths--It Just Feels Right!

Paul grinned with anticipation as he wondered how Tim would react to his next request. "Tim, here's a pen. What hand do you normally sign your name with?"

"I'm right handed," affirmed Tim.

"Great! Now sign your name on the cover of your Life Matches book under where it says 'It Feels Right' using your LEFT hand. Be sure to leave some room to do it again underneath it in a moment," directed Paul as he watched anxiously to see if Tim would follow his instructions.

Reluctantly, Tim shifted the pen to his left hand and paused to gain his bearings. He typically used a similar pen for hours every day with his right hand, but now it felt awkward and almost like a foreign object in his left hand. Carefully and firmly he grasped his matchbook, somewhat afraid he might totally miss his mark on the first try, and as slowly as a kindergartner, he began to write Tim Davis in a nearly legible scrawling hand. Tim snickered at how long it took to complete this seemly simple task and at how unidentifiable his own name looked on the little matchbook.

"Boy, your matchbook is a lie. It says 'It Feels Right!' on the front cover and nothing could be farther from the truth. That could not have felt more wrong to me," jested Tim.

"Well, let's see if we can get to the truth of the exercise then. Go ahead and sign your name below the first example using your RIGHT hand."

Tim quickly and effortlessly complied with Paul's request and with a little hint of pride at his accomplishment said, "Now that feels right!" He admired the familiar name that he had signed so often, especially in his new leadership role, and he compared it to its distant cousin above.

"See, Tim, you have just experienced what it feels like to do something from an area of strength versus an area of weakness. Did you happen to wake up one morning and 'decide' to learn to write using your right hand?"

"Not that I remember. I've always been right handed as far as I know."

"That's exactly my point. You were most likely born with your right handedness. From the moment you first experimented with a writing instrument, maybe even your first crayon, you decided that using your right hand 'just feels right.'"

Tim nodded his agreement partially humoring Paul, but also actually accepting his point.

"Now if you broke your right hand or if you really decided to practice every day for a couple of hours a day, do you think you would ever become as comfortable writing using your left hand as you are right now using your right hand?"

"I sincerely hope I could get to at least something that someone else could read."

"I'm sure you could with enough practice and coaching, but do you think it would ever come as naturally and feel as 'right' as using your right hand?" asked Paul.

"I doubt it."

"So, can you see how this might apply to our other job and life-related tasks?" queried Paul, hoping Tim could make the connection.

"So what you're saying is that just like using your natural handedness to write with, using your strengths just comes naturally and no matter how hard you try you will most likely never be able to improve a weakness to the level of your strength," surmised Tim as he chewed over this thought along with the remaining half of his grilled chicken sandwich.

"Yes, that's true. You see, doing what feels natural or easy for you is a clue to one or more of your strengths. It just feels right!

"Building on your strengths to make them even stronger is going to be easier and probably more successful and certainly more fun than fighting your natural tendencies and abilities to try to improve one of your weaknesses.

"In some areas of weakness, you might never get to a passing grade no matter how hard you try, so maybe the smart thing to do is to try to manage around the weakness rather than make a futile effort to improve the weakness."

Tim was a little taken aback by Paul's last point and asked, "So are you suggesting that we should just throw in the towel on something that doesn't feel right and admit failure and not even try to improve? That doesn't sound like a path to success to me!"

"No, not at all," explained Paul. "What I meant is to be realistic and to appreciate that we only have so much time in any given day, and on this planet for that matter, to complete our life's mission. We must decide the wisest investments of our time and energies, so that we can become the most effective human beings that we were uniquely designed to be. Let me give you another example.

"Knowing you're a football fan, what if your life's dream was to play in the NFL? Is it realistic to think that you could realize your dream?"

Tim, who had dreamed that dream as a child and then as a high school football star, responded, "Well it depends on a lot of factors and might be a long-shot, but maybe."

"Agreed, but if you are 40 percent smaller and slower than the average NFL player are your chances better or worse of starting in the NFL?"

"That would make it extremely unlikely," Tim relented.

"And it wouldn't matter how positive your thinking was. No matter how much you desired it to happen or how hard you practiced, you would probably never make the team, would you?"

"Not if you are small and slow with so much competition."

"Agreed, and all the time you spent positively thinking, working out, practicing and trying to make the team, while it might have been fun for you, it wouldn't have yielded the results you desired, so in some sense it was wasted efforts. Now what if instead you also knew you were a genius who had the ability to invent the next artificial heart that would save thousands of lives and make you unbelievably wealthy and famous, but you never invented it because you were so busy practicing for the NFL?"

"Well, I guess you could say I was living my dream, for better or worse, while I was doing it and I would hope I would have enough time left in this life to still be able to invent the artificial heart and watch the NFL team I would buy with my riches from having invented it!" mused Tim.

"That works if you last long enough, but what if...."

"I died?" Tim finished Paul's sentence. "Then I guess it wouldn't matter to me anymore and the rest of the heart patients would be out of luck."

Tim had actually been enjoying the lunch and discussion up to this point, but now his shirt collar felt a little tight and the room seemed too warm. "What if I died?" was back, front and center in his mind.

Life Matches: Fire Up Your Life!

Tim paid the check and told Paul that he thought the information was certainly worth presenting at the managers' summit meeting, but he needed to return to his office for his conference call.

Paul sensed that something had hit a nerve with Tim and thanked him for listening. Paul slid a new copy of *StrengthsFinder 2.0* across the table to Tim.

"Tim, before you go, will you consider doing four favors for me? The first is to browse through the *StrengthsFinder 2.0* book and then take the online assessment. Also, keep your Life Matches with you in your pocket for the next 20 days as a reminder to use your strengths, gifts and talents daily. And finally, favor four is if you do learn something interesting about yourself, then we can get together for another lunch soon and I will continue my Life Matches presentation.

"You'll notice that there are some more blank spaces on your Life Matches book that I would like to help you fill in if you'll give me some more of your time. I'll even buy lunch again next time. Deal?"

"I'll take the test and we'll see what happens," offered Tim somewhat reluctantly.

Chapter 5: More Signs of Weakness

The next day Tim arrived at work at his usual 6:50 a.m. and saw his copy of *StrengthsFinder 2.0* and the printed Life Matches worksheets on his desk. He flipped through the book and unsealed and scratched off his access code for the online strengths assessment.

Tim logged onto his computer and saw that he already had 23 new e-mail messages waiting for him in his inbox file. He decided the prospect of an online survey sounded much more inviting than starting to fight e-mail fires, so he entered the StrengthsFinder address into his web browser.

A few minutes later he was reviewing his online results in the form of a personal *StrengthsFinder 2.0* Strengths Insight Guide. Tim's strengths were Achiever, WOO (Winning Others Over), Competition, Maximizer, and Strategic. As Tim read the definition of each term he smiled more than once as each description closely matched his personality. What surprised Tim was which traits were not on his report. Missing characteristics were Discipline, Focus, Analytical, Command and Responsibility, which were the skills he thought he used most in his new role as the director of sales. To sum up Tim, he was an "Influencer," who is someone who can sell others on ideas, takes charge, speaks up, and has the ability to get an idea widely adopted--all of which seemed to apply nicely to his role as a director of sales.

The worksheets Paul also left for Tim to complete seemed simple enough to finish, until he started to write in the blanks. Then the questions turned out to be anything but simple for him as he began to really think about his answers to "What Fires Me Up!" and "What Fizzles Me Out." When Tim was finally finished, he read and signed the pledge that was also included.

Tim's answers to Paul's worksheets—

Fires You Up! or Fizzles You Out—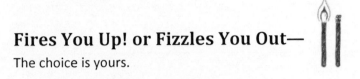
The choice is yours.

Describe how you feel when you are doing something that makes you feel "Fired Up!"

I know I am doing something that fires me up when:

I love doing every minute of it. When time seems to fly by. When I don't have to think about doing the process of something, it just sort of happens and my body and mind are acting together perfectly and naturally. When I feel like I am in my natural element.

List three words that best describe your feeling of being "Fired Up!"

1) Natural

2) Fun

3) Satisfying

Describe how you feel when you are doing something that makes you feel "Fizzled Out."

I know I am doing something that fizzles me out when:

I HATE every minute of doing it. I can't get started or put off doing it. It's just not my thing. I feel bored doing it. When I feel that doing something is NOT me.

List three words that best describe your feeling of being "Fizzled Out."

1) Drained

2) Unchallenged

3) Bored

List the five activities that take up the majority of your time and energy during a typical **work day**. Rank how "Fired Up!" or "Fizzled Out" you feel while thinking about doing each activity.

<u>**Fired Up!**</u>   <u>**Neutral**</u>   <u>**Fizzled Out**</u>

1) Fix other peoples' mistakes _____ 1 2 3 4⑤

2) Sales analysis _____ 1 2③4 5

3) Creating a sales strategy _____ ①2 3 4 5

4) Assist and coach my managers _____ 1②3 4 5

5) Create reports for senior management 1 2 3 4⑤

28

List five **non-work** activities that you choose to invest the majority of your time and energy doing.

Fired Up! **Neutral** **Fizzled Out**

1) Spend time with my family _____   1 2 3 ④ 5

2) Watch TV _____   1 2 ③ 4 5

3) Read _____   1 2 ③ 4 5

4) Golf _____   1 2 ③ 4 5

5) Church committee _____   1 ② 3 4 5

Total your scores for your five work and non-work activities that you scored above. The lower your score, the more "Fired Up!" your main activities make you feel. A score of a perfect 10 means your life is fully ablaze!

My Score: __31__

Repeat this exercise with the next five work and non-work activities that take the most of your time. Keep repeating the exercise until most of your common work and non-work activities are ranked. Be sure to review a few of your daily to-do lists to find regularly occurring activities.

List three ways that you will adjust your **work life** to allow you to invest more time and energy doing activities that fire you up!

1) Schedule time to call on customers and to socialize with them.

2) Set aside time to review and develop the sales strategy.

3) Focus on coaching.

List three ways that you will adjust your **non-work life** to allow you to invest more time and energy doing activities that fire you up!

1) Find fun things to do with my family.

2) Watch less TV.

3) Find a real hobby.

List three ways that you will adjust your **work life** which will allow you to reduce or to stop investing time and energy doing activities that fizzle you out at work.

1) Encourage people to fix their own

mistakes.

2) Delegate some report preparation.

3) Leave at 6:00 p.m. or earlier most nights.

List three ways that you will adjust your **non-work life** which will allow you to reduce or to stop investing time and energy doing activities that fizzle you out when you are not working.

1) Learn how to help manage Savannah's AD/HD.

2) Schedule a weekly date night with Joanne.

3) Find my faith.

List three people who could help you to achieve working more "Fired Up!"

1) Paul

2) Meg

3) Carlos

List three people who could help you to achieve living a more "Fired Up!" life outside of work.

1) Joanne

2) Rodney

3) God

4) My Fired Up Life Pledge

Beginning today, I pledge to seek out ways to live my life and to do my work so that I use my God-given strengths so that   I feel "Fired Up!" I will not allow my weaknesses to hinder me from enjoying a "Fired Up!" life, by draining my energy and fizzling me out. I will discover ways to manage around my weaknesses so that they are not factors in achieving my goals and living the satisfied life that is uniquely mine. I will seek guidance through prayer and from those I love and respect to help me achieve and maintain my "Fired Up!" life. I claim the gift of my strengths and talents and pledge to use them for their highest good.

I promise to carry my Life Matches with me for at least the next 20 days as a reminder of my commitment to live a life which is truly "Fired Up!"

Signed:_____ Date: March 20, 2010

Why was it so hard to think of five non-work activities? thought Tim. Arguing with Joanne and struggling with Savannah's AD/HD seemed like the activities that took most of his non-work energy. He hardly spent any time with little Stephanie and she was only going to be little once. Tim wondered--Am I being really honest to classify my few hours at home as spending time with my family? It's been a long time since I've done something I really enjoy, just for the fun of doing it.

He worked through the exercise and was somewhat surprised by his answers. How can I be near the top of the career ladder and feel fizzled out most of the time? Tim wondered.

He remembered how excited he had been when he was first asked by his regional vice president to accept the additional responsibilities of being the director of sales. Tim had been successful first as an account executive and then in his past sales management roles. Mostly, he had always enjoyed a feeling of confidence in his abilities, knowing he was probably still the best salesperson on his team.

I guess I miss the daily thrill of the sales hunt and closing really big deals, Tim surmised. Seeing clients and closing deals didn't even make my top five daily activities. How did that happen? My real value to our organization is when I'm leading by example in the field and helping my local sales managers and account executives close business deals and build lasting relationships with our customers. Socializing with customers is also absent on my top five list. Now most of my time is in data analysis, forecasting, budgeting and dealing with other people's problems. Definitely not my strong suits, reflected Tim.

I don't mind being in charge, but I feel much happier presenting with PowerPoint than crunching with Excel. Helping our customers see the tremendous value my company can bring to them and solving their problems are what gives me the greatest satisfaction. That and winning!

That's the funny thing about senior leadership. It's hard to know when you really win. There's always another budget mountain to climb and we probably don't take enough time to celebrate each summit we reach, let alone enjoy the journey itself, he surmised. It seems like I'm living my life in fast forward lately, maybe burning the candle at both ends and the middle is causing me to fizzle out.

Tim was brought back from his thoughts the moment his desk phone rang. The upside of caller ID was being able to know who was calling. The downside of knowing who was calling was that sometimes you did not want to answer the call. Tim certainly felt like this was one of those downside times….

Two amazingly short hours later, Tim had the now familiar burning in his chest and the bitter acid taste in his mouth as he finally hung up the phone. The discussion had started with yet another irate customer concerning an issue and had resulted in a hastily arranged conference call with MegaAds' head of operations and the account executive. A tense call with Tim's boss concluded the ordeal.

I might as well stop wearing this business suit and start wearing a fire hat and raincoat with as many stupid fires as I have to put out, Tim imagined. This business runs on details and if one silly check box is not checked, then the whole system starts to spiral out of control. Account executives are almost paralyzed with paperwork in our system and we are forcing them to be perfect data entry experts. . . certainly not one of their strengths!

The thought of the word "strengths" made Tim smile as he remembered his list of what Fires Me Up and Fizzles Me Out. Putting out other peoples' fires and conference calls are certainly fizzlers for me, he mused.

Tim typed an e-mail to Paul, "Ready to hear the rest of your story whenever you are. –T"

Paul promptly responded with an electronic appointment for Tim's calendar for 11:30 a.m. the next day.

Chapter 6: The Rest of the Story

Tim sat down at an empty booth at the back of the office cafeteria. He was a few minutes early and did not see Paul yet. Tim used the spare free moments to review his answers and to try to attach some actionable meaning to them.

Tim was prepared for this meeting and had brought his *StrengthsFinder 2.0* results and his completed worksheets on what Fires Me Up! or Fizzles Me Out and, of course, the book of matches with his name on the cover. Tim had been carrying these matches around since his last meeting with Paul.

Paul greeted Tim with a broad smile and hardy handshake, "Thanks again for agreeing to help me prep for the sales managers' summit meeting. I know you probably have a lot on your plate."

Tim smiled and sniffed a confirmation to being extremely busy. "If you only knew," he lamented.

"Oh, I probably do know. It's only been a couple of months since I began my director of sales recovery program!" jested Paul.

Paul and Tim passed through the cafeteria line and found a table somewhat away from the rest of the lunchtime diners. After they sat down with their food, it only took a moment for Paul to ask, "Were you able to find the time to take the *StrengthsFinder 2.0* test and work through the Fires Me Up!-Fizzles Me Out worksheets?"

"Yes. It was actually an enlightening exercise. I think the test pretty well identified at least some of my strengths, but your worksheets were another story."

"Well, I guess that's good news. What were your categories from the test?"

"I could sure see why I gravitated into sales. My strengths are Achiever, WOO (Winning Others Over), Competition, Maximizer, and Strategic. These were not really surprising for me, except I thought several of the other types listed in the book were equally good descriptions. I wonder why they didn't show up in my profile report?"

"We all have a combination of multiple strengths traits. The test picks a person's top five traits to highlight, but certainly one has many more. That's where your Life Matches come in! Did you happen to bring your matchbook with you?"

"I did," boasted Tim as he shifted in his seat to retrieve his matchbook from deep in his pocket. "It's starting to look a little ragged, kind of like the way I feel. Are you sure these are not mood matches?"

Paul chuckled, "I don't think so, but I'll make a note of that to use for the next summit meeting. Okay, now open your book and on the inside of the flap, can you please write each of your strength traits?"

Tim nodded and pulled his Monte Blanc pen from his shirt pocket and neatly wrote, using his natural right hand, Achiever, WOO, Competition, Maximizer and Strategic on the little inside cover of the matchbook.

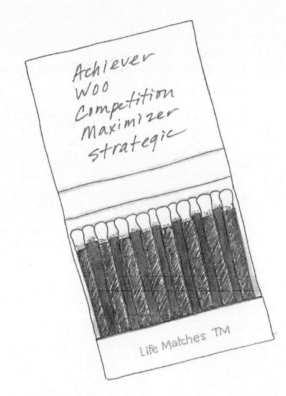

"Perfect penmanship," encouraged Paul. "Now let me tell you the rest of the Life Matches story."

"Each one of these matches represents a unique, God-given gift, talent and strength. Just like you have a strength in writing with your right hand, you have been gifted with many other natural talents. These talents make up not only who you are, but also they represent your innate capacity or potential to become the ultimate you that only you can become. The challenge is to learn how to maximize your strengths and how to manage around your weaknesses."

"Are you telling me that I should play with matches?" joked Tim.

"Well, I'm not suggesting that you should 'play' with your Life Matches, as much as I am recommending that you undertake a daily Life Matches' exercise program. The good news is that you get to design a personal strategy to help you use, develop, explore and discover each match in your book. The more practice living a 'Fired Up' life the more natural it feels and pretty soon, living 'Fired Up' will just become the way you live your life. Now let's talk for a minute about the chemistry of fire."

"Do we have to? I've never claimed to have a strength in science," cautioned Tim.

"I promise not to get too technical. In order to have fire or combustion you need the right mix of three elements. First you need fuel of some sort. Second, you need air and lastly, you need an ignition source, or a spark." Using Tim's pen, Paul wrote the following elements on his napkin and turned it to face Tim.

1) Fuel of some sort

2) Air

3) Ignition source, or a spark

"With Life Matches you can think of the fuel as being made up of your talents, strengths, knowledge and life experiences. Your passions are a fuel additive that adds extra power to your life fuel."

Tim nodded his understanding, so Paul continued. "Air for Life Matches is simply, time. The ignition or spark to light a Life Match can come from many different sources. You can get into close proximity to someone else using one of his or her Life Matches and it can help you light one of your own matches. There are sometimes spontaneous sparks caused by the environment, situation or circumstances you experience. Sometimes it takes lots of plain hard work and practice, just like rubbing two sticks together, to finally spark one of your Life Matches."

"So, let me see if I follow you. Each match is something I can naturally do well and that's the fuel. I need time to use each match and lastly, I need something to get me started?" confirmed Tim.

"Well done! That's exactly right," Paul said enthusiastically. "It sounds like you are ready for a review." From his portfolio Paul produced bullet-pointed PowerPoint slides that he was planning to include in his presentation for the managers' summit meeting. He reviewed each of the points with Tim:

- Your book of Life Matches is a physical reminder of the strengths you were born with.
- I'm sorry to say that you don't get to choose your strengths.
- Only you have the power to choose if, when and how you will use and develop your strengths.
- You can take a lifetime to uncover and discover each of your Life Match strengths.
- It takes lots of patient practice to learn how and when to use a Life Match strength effectively.
- Only you get to decide if you choose to light a Life Match.

- Life Match mastery comes when you learn the best way to spark each Life Match into action and how you can keep the fuel or passion feeding your flame.

Tim carefully followed Paul's explanation and presentation. From time to time he quickly glanced at his little book of Life Matches on the table in front of him. Finally, he picked up the book of matches and opened the cover to read his five strengths written on the inside. He took a moment to ponder the neat rows of matches in silence and then said, "I really like your matches metaphor. My guess is that it will resonate with many of our managers. My challenge is not in accepting that what you're saying is true, as much as in trying to figure out how I can use what you're teaching me. Your theory is great, but it's my execution that is a challenge. After working on your worksheets, I'm afraid I am stuck in the dark and could sure use some light. Let's walk through my Fires Me Up and Fizzles Me Out worksheets. I'm anxious to get your take on my answers."

Chapter 7: It's Okay to Play with Life Matches

"Paul, I'm a pretty good sales strategist and I'm also good at coming up with new ideas and solutions as to how we can best sell our products," said Tim. "When I'm planning our quarterly sales strategies with my local sales managers, my juices really get flowing and I feel like I'm in the zone. What might seem like long and boring meetings to some, seem to take no time at all to me. In fact, when I'm in those meetings, time seems to stop. During those meetings, it's not unusual for me to look down at my watch and see that four or five hours have flown by. I really look forward to those planning meetings."

Paul listened intently and nodded his understanding. "So planning and strategy are areas that you both enjoy and are good at. As I think back on the times we've worked together, I would definitely agree with you. Because you are good at something, enjoy it and are recognized by others as being talented in that area, you can be pretty certain that you have found not only something that fires you up, but also something that allows you to use one or more of your Life Matches. How much of your typical week do you think you set aside to use your strategic strengths?"

"You know we have the quarterly planning meetings and we spend time annually preparing for budget presentations," replied Tim.

"Sure, but how many hours or days per year do you think you get to truly use these strategic Life Matches that you enjoy using so much? Do you get to use them outside of work also?"

Tim thought for a while and then said quietly, "I guess I get to plan at work about three weeks out of the whole year. I guess I also get to use those skills when I participate in a long-range planning committee for my church."

"So about six percent of your total working time is spent fired up planning a sales strategy and a little outside time at your church. That leaves you with 94 percent of the rest of your work time. What else about your job as director of sales gets you in your zone?"

"I also like looking for new ways for our company to make more money," interjected Tim enthusiastically. "I get a great sense of satisfaction when I dream up a new way to package our products or a sales promotion or event that brings in some big bucks. To answer your question in advance, I probably get to do that another week out of the year."

"So what you're telling me is that you are fired up about one out of 12 months or eight percent of the time at work. Is that about right?"

"When you put it that way, it's no wonder I feel like I'm not having a lot of fun most of the time in my new role."

"I'll be the first one to agree with you from first-hand experience. Being the director of sales for an entire state is no easy task," reassured Paul. "But the job is what it is. Every job has its good and bad elements. The interesting thing is that it's all based upon individual perceptions which judge each job's tasks as being something which fires you up or fizzles you out. One person's pain is a different person's passion. Each of us gets to decide, based on our perceptions, feelings, what makes our lives feel successful, fulfilled, satisfied, meaningful and significant."

"So what if I have a natural aptitude for something, but I absolutely hate doing it?"

"Have you been reading my autobiography, Tim?" joked Paul. "That is exactly why I chose to take on the challenges of this new training role and give up being the director of sales. I feel like I did a pretty decent job as the director. But at the end of most days I went home drained and exhausted. Even though I had won our highest management award, I sometimes felt a little like I was an imposter and that at any moment I might be discovered as a fraud. Paranoia and fear can be effective motivators for a while, but they drain you of any joy and sense of satisfaction from your accomplishments."

"You certainly were a terrific director! So good that I really considered not pitching to be your replacement since you would be such a hard act to follow," Tim said emphatically.

"Thanks. That's kind of you to say."

"So can I ask you a personal question, Paul?"

Paul nodded.

"What made you decide to finally change roles?"

"It was the winter solstice, the longest night of the year. I like to stay up late and reflect on the past year and to start thinking about my

New Year's resolutions. That night, I went back to my first personal journal entry for that year and read forward until I came to the last page. To be perfectly honest, it was not easy to read. It was not a happy story by a happy guy and if it continued, I couldn't see it ending happily ever after. So that night, I picked up my copy of *StrengthsFinder 2.0* and took the online survey. I spent the next three months really looking at what fired me up and what fizzled me out.

"I like to make lists, so I kept a running list of daily to-do tasks and before each task I put a plus or a minus to indicate how I felt about anticipating doing it. If I was looking forward to it or at least not procrastinating or avoiding doing it, it received a plus and if I felt like I had to do it and it was going to be a drag doing it, I gave it a minus. Then I did the same thing after I completed each task, only I marked the plus or minus after the to-do list entry based on how I felt while I was actually doing the task. At the end of each day, I looked at which tasks were two pluses or only one plus and then I evaluated the minuses. I quickly started to see a pattern. I was spending and enjoying more of my time teaching, coaching and developing people than I was managing inventory, pricing, policies, systems, and the other nuts and bolts of directing our sales organization.

"What I discovered was that even though I was reasonably good at doing most of the director's tasks that I had assigned at least one minus to, I didn't receive any emotional benefit while I was doing them or even when I had finished doing them.

"I started thinking that in our advertising world, when we make a mistake on a client's commercial schedule, we run a makegood commercial to make up for our mistake. We get to do it over again and make it right. In life, it's a live performance and we don't get any makegoods. It's a one- shot deal, and I believe we should make the most out of every second we are given. If I died tonight on the way home from work, I would hate to have had my last thoughts been that my last day on this earth was a total waste of time, filled with doing stupid things I hated doing."

A cold jolt of electricity shot through Tim's body at the mention and thought of death.

"I know what you mean," murmured Tim over the rim of his glass of water as he quickly took a sip.

"It naturally takes some time to adjust to any new role, but if you feel like perhaps it's more than just new-guy-adjustment- jitters, then maybe you could try my pluses and minuses to-do list exercise for a while. Also, don't forget to list your non-work activities too. Sometimes knowing when you're fired up at play can be excellent clues to how you can play more at work," suggested Paul.

"Play? Who has any time or energy left for play?" whined Tim with a note of self-pity.

"No one in leadership just happens to find time for relaxation and play. They have to make it a priority and an appointment, just like everything else on their to-do list. But the old saying of all work and no play makes Paul a dull and very unhappy boy has surely proven to be true for me. What do you like to do to relax and have fun?"

"When any Indianapolis team is winning, I like to watch them play on TV. On the rare occasions when I can put my game all together, I enjoy a round of golf, but I don't play often enough to keep a good game in my bag."

"What do you enjoy doing as a family?"

"Just the normal, boring stuff, I guess. With two little girls, it's been mainly Joanne's area of expertise. I kind of feel in the way and out of their loop most of the time."

Paul paused and thought for a moment, then said, "Tim, I know your family is very important to you. I'm going to jump on my soap box for a minute with your permission and prescribe without a license. Can I do that?"

Tim nodded his permission.

"Your girls need their daddy and need to see daddy making them a priority and making them feel important. Joanne needs to feel that also as well as feel supported and appreciated. I know from experience and hours of marriage counseling that it's up to each of us to choose to engage daily into these key relationships and to give them the time, energy and attention they need to flourish. If not, our relationships become as withered and dead as a plant you forgot to water for months. It doesn't happen naturally for us Type-A doers. We have to make it happen and practice until it becomes a habit. I've always found that I tended to give all my time and energy to work and to people who mean the least to me and I had very little left for the people who would cry at my funeral, if you know what I mean."

Paul's words hit Tim's heart like a hammer, breaking its self-centered and self-pitying coating of ice. He quickly rubbed his moist eyes to avoid revealing tears. I hope someone would cry at my funeral, thought Tim.

"You know, you're making a lot of sense. I appreciate you taking the time to talk about this stuff and I do value your opinion. Let me have some time to think about all you've been saying and I'll buy lunch later in the week and you can show me the rest of your presentation on Life Matches for the managers' summit meeting."

"Hey, I'm sorry if I got a little passionate with you, but in case you couldn't tell, I really feel strongly that this stuff is very important. And I'll be happy to let you buy me lunch," answered Paul.

Chapter 8: Home for Dinner

At 5:10 p.m. Tim signed off his computer and spent the next 25 minutes reworking and prioritizing his to-do list for tomorrow, something he had not done in a long time. He also carefully placed a plus or a minus in front of each task's priority as to how he felt about doing them. Tim's list looked like the following:

To Do

++ 1 A Work w/ local managers on managers' summit agenda

--2 A Performance reviews

- -3 A Prep for region conference call-budget short-fall justification

++A Lunch with Volksman's Automall

-+B Check NFL inventory and average rate

- -B Discussion on mandatory HR training

- -A Approve coaching plan for Collins

‡+B Coach Sullivan

--C Schedule meeting with attorney

--C Financial review

Much to the surprise of Joanne, Tim arrived home before the girls and she had sat down to dinner. Perhaps even more shocking to Joanne was the sense that he appeared to actually be in a reasonably good mood.

"What are you doing home so early?" asked Joanne as she accepted a cheek peck from Tim in the kitchen.

"I've been thinking a lot lately about some stuff and I'm trying to make some better choices," said Tim.

"Ooookay," she said tentatively.

"Don't worry; it's nothing crazy or drastic. I just think I've been living to work instead of working to live lately and I need to rebalance my life a bit," reassured Tim as he sorted through the day's mail.

"Is there something you're not telling me? Does this have anything to do with your trip to the hospital? Tim, are you having an affair?" blurted Joanne in rapid fire as her eyes filled with tears and she wrung a dishtowel in her hands.

Joanne's questions hit Tim like a boxer's combination blows. He took two steps backward and sat down at the kitchen table, stunned. His silence was torturous to a now frozen and crying Joanne, whose questions still hovered over Tim's head like little executioners awaiting their chance to murder and to destroy their family.

Tim swallowed hard on the vile acid that his stomach erupted into his mouth as his mind raced as to how best to answer Joanne's accusations. He took a deep breath and rubbed his now throbbing head. His emotions were a toxic mix of anger, frustration, fear, loneliness, indignation and guilt. He felt like his life was now completely spiraling dangerously out of control. "God help me!" he prayed to himself.

Interpreting his silence as an admission of guilt to her worst nightmare, she tensely spat out, "That's it, isn't it, Tim? You are having an affair!"

Joanne's words slapped Tim back into the present with some clarity. "JoJo, no, I am not having an affair," Tim said quietly and deliberately, as he tried desperately to remain somewhat calm and to regain control of himself.

Joanne's eyes locked on Tim's as she defensively sought to detect the truth of Tim's words that she so desperately wanted to be true. Having never known Tim to lie, she exhaled.

Through the tears Joanne loudly sobbed, "Then why have you checked out so much from your family? Tim, your daughters hardly even know you anymore and you and I are more like roommates than husband and wife!"

Finding some courage and strength, Tim stood up and moved to hug Joanne. Quietly he said directly into Joanne's ear, "You're right, and I'm so sorry for that," as Tim's tears now wet Joanne's hair and shoulder. "I've let my job become the sole focus of my life and you and the girls have suffered for it," admitted Tim. "JoJo, there is no one else in my life but you and the girls. I love you and the kids with all my heart and I'm going to make some better choices with where I invest my time and energies from now on. I promise!"

Hugging, crying and reconnecting in the way that was long absent, they were just together in that moment standing in their kitchen when a puzzled eight-year-old Stephanie walked in and seeing them both, asked, "What's wrong, you guys?"

Tim just smiled though his tears and held out his arm in invitation to Stephanie to join their hug and reassuringly said, "Nothing honey. Daddy's just finally home for dinner."

Chapter 9: Rekindling the Family Fires

As the girls played somewhere in the house, Tim walked into the living room and sat on the couch next to Joanne who was watching a home decorating show on television.

"JoJo, can we please talk about some of the things I've been thinking about?" he asked as he slid his arm behind her and she snuggled closer to him. Joanne raised the remote control and turned off the television and said, "Sure."

"Paul has been working on this presentation for our managers' summit meeting and he asked me to look it over for him. He calls it Life Matches." he proceeded to pull out his somewhat worn book of matches from his pocket and handed it to her.

He explained what he had learned so far from Paul about lighting up your strengths and managing around your natural weaknesses. She listened intently and asked some questions to make sure that she understood what was obviously very important to him.

After about 20 minutes of discussion, which was certainly the longest conversation that Tim and Joanne had shared in months, she said, "It sounds like you're really on to something here. You've definitely got some things to work out about your new job. But what I'm most curious about is how are you planning to use some of your matches to warm up your time with us?"

"I've been thinking a lot about that. One thing I will promise you is that I am going to try very hard at keeping you and the girls a higher priority than my job."

Joanne couldn't contain a snicker of experience-based disbelief.

"No, really, JoJo. I know I've said it before, but after my little hospital episode, I've realized life is short and precious. Paul said you should give your best work to the people who will cry at your funeral. I'm really going to work on that," swore Tim.

"Honey, I know you mean what you're saying," said Joanne, "but what are you going to commit to doing to make this time different?"

"You know me. I work best when I have a plan. And while it may not seem heartfelt to you, I am going to make appointments in my to-do list for you, Savannah, Stephanie and even our poor neglected dog, Walter."

"You mean you are going to have your people call our people to schedule an appointment?" sarcastically chided Joanne.

"No, I mean I am leaving the office on a normal basis, no later than six o'clock. And I am going to leave the office at the office and try not to bring work home, especially on the weekends."

"That sounds all well and good, but can you really do that and not get behind at work?"

"It all depends on how successful I am at using my matches!"

"So when you're here, you are really going to try to be here for us and not locked away in your study or lost in a ballgame?"

"That's what I'm saying. I want to start out by sharing some quality time with you and each of the girls. What would you like for us to begin with?"

Joanne exhaled a long breath and looked directly into Tim's eyes and said, "If you're serious, I would like to book some time with you to go to couples therapy. I think we need some professional help to strengthen our marriage and relationship first."

Tim was caught off guard by Joanne's request, but he could see by the look on her face that she was not only serious, but was testing Tim's words by asking for tangible action. Taking Joanne's hand in his, he looked deeply into her eyes and smiled and said, "If you feel like we need it, then we do and I'll be happy to be there with you."

A wave of disbelief was washed away by relief at his words and she hugged and kissed him deeply as tears streaked her cheeks. As they broke their embrace, Tim called loudly for the girls, "Savannah, Stephanie, can you please come here for a minute?"

"What?" yelled Savannah.

"Please come here, I want to talk with you both."

Savannah and Stephanie eventually entered the living room followed by Walter, the dog. The girls looked around the room apprehensively at their parents and seeing Joanne wiping her eyes and blowing her nose with a tissue, asked, "What's wrong with Mom? Are we in trouble?"

"I'm fine," reassured Joanne.

Tim laughed, "No you're not in trouble. I just wanted to ask you both a question. Come sit on the couch and talk to us."

Savannah sat on the arm of the couch and Stephanie climbed onto Joanne's lap.

"Girls, Daddy wants to plan some time for us to each do something together. Just you and me, having some fun. Can you help me come up with some ideas?" asked Tim.

"Just you and me? What about Mom and Stephanie?" asked Savannah trying to understand what was going on.

"They'll get to pick something too."

"Like what?" asked Stephanie.

"Like whatever you want, within reason."

"So we could go ride our bikes together every day?"

"I don't know about every day, babe, but is biking something you would like for us to do?" asked Tim.

"Yeah, that would be fun!" bubbled Stephanie with a huge smile.

"Okay. How about you, Savannah?" asked Tim.

Savannah bit the nail of her first finger and looked down at the floor. "I don't know."

"That's all right, Munchkin. You don't have to decide right now, but think about it and let me know what you come up with, okay?"

"Okay, Daddy," said Savannah, "are we done?"

"Sure. Stephanie, we'll go for a bike ride after dinner tomorrow night if the weather's good."

"Yeah!" said Stephanie as she lunged across the couch and gave Tim a huge, heartfelt hug, then jumped off the couch and followed Savannah out of the room.

"It's been forever since you've ridden a bike, Tim," warned Joanne.

"You're right. But you know, I used to really like riding." said Tim, "and I can sure use the exercise. Speaking of exercise, Walter, do you want to go for a walk?"

With a mighty basset "WOOF!" and rapid wagging of the whole back half of his body, Walter let the whole house know that yes, he did want to go for a walk.

Tim got up from the couch to find Walter's leash and asked Joanne if she wanted to go along. She said she wouldn't want to impose on Walter's time and gave Tim a wink and a smile as she turned on the television.

Chapter 10: The Back of the Book

Tim was eager to share with Paul all the progress he had made since they last met, and he had hardly touched his lunch by the time Paul finished with his. Paul wiped his mouth with his napkin and congratulated Tim on all his hard work, insights and plans.

"You are turning out to be my star learner," said Paul enthusiastically. "I think you're ready for the next part of my Life Matches story. Did you happen to bring your Life Matches with you?" he asked, hoping Tim had remembered to bring them.

"I don't leave home without them!" said Tim with a satisfied smile as he set them on the table.

"The back cover of the matches is where you get a chance to write a short life motto to summarize you and your life at your most fired up. Think of this as your life condensed down to a billboard or t-shirt or better yet what you would like written as your epitaph on your headstone."

Producing his own, well-worn book of Life Matches from his pants pocket, Paul said, "Here's mine. 'Learn it, Live it, Share the Spark!' I consider myself a life-long work-in-progress and am always learning new things. Once I learn something and I live with it a while and find it to be helpful and true, I cannot wait to share this newfound knowledge with someone else to spark up their life."

"I want my epitaph to read simply, 'Mission Accomplished!' So, how about you Tim? How do you want to be remembered?" asked Paul.

Tim looked at the back cover of his Life Matches which was printed with "Be Who You Are" on the back.

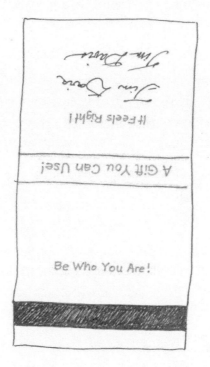

After a long pause Tim said thoughtfully, "This could take some time to get it right."

Paul smiled in agreement and said, "Take all the time you need. You have a lifetime to figure this out. But unless you do the hard work, someone else will choose your epitaph for you after you are gone and who knows what they might come up with!"

Tim chuckled at the thought of what Joanne and the girls might compose and decided that it certainly would be in the history's best interest for him to decide on an epitaph that he could live with, or rather rest in peace with for eternity.

Chapter 11: Warning Label

"Another topic I want to go over in the presentation at the managers' summit meeting is that a warning label should probably come with your Life Matches," said Paul.

"How so?" inquired Tim.

"You see, life's storms and other people will try to blow out your Life Matches from time to time. Life Matches are a positive light in the world, and many people hate anything that shines a light on the fact that they are choosing not to use their strengths. They especially hate the fact that they have allowed themselves to fizzle out and have chosen to stay that way.

"Seeing someone excel by using their strengths makes some people feel jealous, bad and sometimes lazy. Some people get angry because they think that life is not fair, because they were not gifted with a particular strength.

"Instead of doing the hard work of figuring out their own strengths, they spend their whole life's energy trying to extinguish other peoples' aspirations at the first sign of smoke. These kinds of people are often called critics. Very few statues have ever been built to honor their achievements.

"Some other people have become comfortable living in the cold darkness of their fears and failures and become more afraid of the light of someone else's success.

"The real secret of Life Matches is that only you can choose to extinguish one of your own Life Matches. Once they are burning brightly, a Life Match is indestructible as long as you continue to provide it with fuel, which are your passions, and air, which is time.

"So don't worry when the world huffs and puffs and tries to blow your Life Matches out. Just keep on using your strengths and build a brighter and stronger flame through practice," taught Paul.

"I think I know a few huffers and puffers myself," volunteered Tim.

Paul smiled and said that the world is full of them. He went on to explain about another potential Life Match hazard. "While only you can choose to light and extinguish one of your reusable Life Matches, you have to be very careful to choose the right time and match to light in a given situation.

"We all know that striking a match near gasoline can be an explosive situation. The same thing can happen if you use one of your Life Matches at an inappropriate time or in an inappropriate way," he warned.

"Are you saying, for example, that my strength of being decisive at work might cause Joanne to suddenly explode if I use it at home?" asked Tim.

Paul nodded his agreement and mutual understanding of Tim's comment and then continued, "The other real danger is over developing one particular strength or Life Match at the expense of the rest of the matches in your book.

"This results in a person who only has a hammer in his tool belt, so he starts to treat everything he sees like a nail. We need to explore and discover all the different matches in our Life Matches book that we've been gifted with. The challenge is to know when and how best to use them.

"Unfortunately, it's a trial-by-fire process and we often get a little burned no matter how careful we are. Playing with our natural fires and becoming fired up the right way at the right time is what the real challenge of living a fired up life is all about."

"So what I hear you saying is that in the wrong circumstances a strength, if wrongly applied, can become a weakness?" questioned Tim.

"Exactly! Life is all about choosing to use the right tool for the right job and making sure your toolbox is full of tools that you're a master at using. Another way to think about it is that you are the painter of your life's masterpiece. Each of your strengths is another color in your pallet of paints. If you only have blue, your painting is not going to have much variety," affirmed Paul.

"Maybe you had better just stick to matches, Paul. You only have an hour to present this whole thing at the managers' summit," teased Tim.

Paul took Tim's point to heart and replied, "I know. I may need to condense this whole story down a bit. I wanted to go into the responsibility we have as parents to keep our children's matches safe and dry until they are old enough to play with them. We need to expose them to as many different life experiences and opportunities as we can while they are young, so that they can try out as many matches in their books as possible, in a well-supervised environment."

"Telling parents to let their kids play with matches might require a legal disclaimer," warned Tim.

"I hadn't considered that. You may be right," agreed Paul chuckling. "Do you know how you can tell if your child may have found a Life Match?"

Not wanting to ruin the certain punch line to follow, Tim shook his head no.

"You look for smoke signals!" blurted Paul with a belly laugh.

"Paul, you may have been giving this whole matches thing way too much thought."

"Don't I know it! But you know, when you watch a child playing, much of the time they are innocently trying out a whole bunch of different skills and are learning where their strengths lie. They don't have much experience at failures or critics, so they are not afraid to try new things. It's a joy to watch, especially when they light up in truly finding a new strength."

"I see your point about parents, but since this is being presented at the managers' summit meeting, what is your advice to managers like me?"

Chapter 12: Managing Matches

Paul smiled broadly and stated, "I'm glad you asked. Managers are similar in some ways to parents. Effective managers lead by example and allow their teams to see them personally fired up by using their strengths. They systematically identify and discuss the different strengths of each person on their team. The manager talks about how they can work together with each person on his or her team to help them to fire up by developing their strengths.

"First, I think it is reasonable to choose one or two areas that are already a person's strengths. Then we should develop an action plan that will strengthen their strengths to their next level of mastery. As managers, we tend to focus our energies and coaching on our people's weaknesses and not on their strengths. I believe the wiser investment of everyone's time is in creating mutually agreeable strengths' development plans and strategies for managing around weaknesses so that they don't become barriers that inhibit achieving our goals. We certainly don't want our weaknesses or the weaknesses of our staff to hold our team back, but we also don't want to invest all of our time and energy in developing an area that may never get much better than passable.

"Say, for example, that your brain is just not wired for math," Paul continued. "The best grade you might reasonably expect is a C and it might not be worth the extra studying and tutoring efforts that it would take to get to a C plus in math. This would be especially true if it meant that you had no time and energy left to work on your gift in English. You would have wasted your true potential if your extra efforts in math resulted in sub-par performance in English. So a reasonable study strategy would be to work hard enough to secure a C in math and invest the extra time to fully develop your language arts skills and receive an A plus in English. Overall, your grade point average is most likely improved. What you want to do is to not give up on math by allowing your natural weakness to become a crutch or an excuse that you use to justify less than your passing potential, thus allowing math to become a subject that is difficult to manage around later in your life.

"As leaders, we need to take an overall grade point average approach to strengths and weaknesses and choose to let our strengths carry the weight of our success and try to just minimize the friction of our weaknesses, by coping or managing around them. We can also take the same approach with the people that we lead and encourage them to practice the same strengths-based strategies."

"That is exactly why we have chosen to restructure our sales force to a team-based sales strategy. The salespeople are so bogged down with details and paperwork, which are typically not strengths of a top salesperson, that they don't have any time or energy left to go out and see our customers and sell something," interjected Tim.

"That's a perfect example!" said Paul. "In the recent past, we might have actually fired a salesperson with the best client relationship skills or perhaps with a strength in prospecting just because she was a total disaster with our back office, post-sale process. By changing the structure to better manage around the salespeoples' weaknesses, we will increase revenue."

"Don't make eagles try to swim?" offered Tim.

"Didn't you just tell me to stick to matches, Mr. Davis?" poked Paul and then continued, "Now, I think you see why I feel this presentation is so timely. We all need to come to a common understanding and share a language of how developing our strengths and managing around our weaknesses can not only make us more successful, but will also add to our individual engagement and ultimately we all have a lot more fun at this game called work. It can be a landmark cultural transformation for our organization!"

"You've certainly convinced me, Paul. I've been plussing and minusing my daily to-do list and I am getting much closer to knowing exactly what fires me up and fizzles me out, both in and outside of work. I really think your little book of Life Matches is helping me. I've decided to make some important changes in the way I'm living my life and I think they will really make a positive difference. Congratulations, I think you've shared a spark!"

"Tim, that is why I chose to do what I do, so you can do what you do better," said Paul with a tremendous sense of satisfaction.

Tim took his pen from his shirt pocket and wrote the following life motto on the back of his book of Life Matches: "Follow me into the light!"

Paul read what Tim wrote and then smiled broadly. As a gesture of graduation, Paul and Tim ceremoniously shook hands.

Chapter 13: Finding Their Wings

Tim was very pleased with his new time choices at home. Joanne and he met a couple of times with a Christian marriage counselor at their church, and they both felt like they were well on the road to recovery with a map to help them get there.

Riding bikes with Stephanie and nightly walks with Walter had reignited a passion for fitness in Tim and resulted in him sleeping better and dropping a few pounds. He cherished the time following behind little Stephanie who often shouted over her shoulder, "Are you back there, Daddy?" He filled with love and pride every time she asked him that question.

He quickly replied, "You bet, Angel Face! Daddy is right here behind you. Keep peddling, you slow-poke!"

Unfortunately his relationship with Savannah remained strained. Trying to keep her on task and organized was a constant struggle. She was unable or unwilling to think of an activity for both of them to share. She tended to prefer to get lost in her own world on the computer or in texting her few friends.

On the way home from a newly-initiated mommy and daddy date night without the girls, Tim and Joanne drove past the little airport near their home. On the airport fence was a sign that read, "Time Flies. Learn to Fly While There's Still Time!" Tim read the sign out loud to Joanne and without really thinking about it said, "You know. I've always dreamed about learning to fly."

Joanne lovingly placed her hand over his and said warmly, "All it takes is time and money, dear. You have the money. Will you make the time?"

The next day Tim called the airport and scheduled what was called a discovery flight. He announced at the dinner table to the family that he was thinking about becoming a pilot.

Both girls chimed in with a loud, "COOL!"

Savannah quickly added, "Daddy, can I please fly with you?"

That sunny Saturday morning, a very nervous Savannah and Tim were introduced to the various controls and systems in a Cessna 172 Skyhawk airplane which the flight school used for training. Their flight instructor, Beth, was a young, recent college graduate who was building flight time as a flight instructor so she could pursue her dream of flying as the captain of an airliner. She spent plenty of time reassuring and calming Savannah and patiently answered her numerous questions as she conducted a preflight inspection of the four- seat airplane.

With Savannah secured in the rear seat and Tim at the controls in the front left seat, Beth talked to Tim and Savannah from the front right seat using the intercom and headsets they all wore.

Once they were aligned facing into the wind on the runway, Beth said, "Tim, we're ready to fly. Slowly but firmly push in the throttle knob all the way and away we go!"

The plane's engine produced maximum thrust and it raced down the runway. Tim felt the control yolk press against his left palm as Beth applied just enough force to bring the nose wheel off the runway and a moment later they were airborne and flying.

Savannah took it all in from the back seat and focused intently as Beth explained about straight and level cruise flight and how the horizon looks out over the dash. The short flight revealed a world that Tim and Savannah had no way of knowing existed. They experienced the freedom and possibilities that only can be seen from a small plane's cockpit. They circled over their house and could see a waving Joanna and Stephanie in their backyard.

Beth uneventfully landed and parked the plane while Tim and Savannah thanked her for sharing her gift of flight.

Savannah sat in the front seat of Tim's car on the ride home and relived the entire flight again and again as Tim drove, only to share the same stories in great detail to Joanne and Stephanie as soon as they arrived home.

"And the best part was the instructor was a girl!" exclaimed Savannah. "Even girls can fly. That was so totally awesome, Daddy! Thank you so much for taking me. Are you really going to learn how to fly?"

"I think so, Munchkin. It was totally awesome!" said Tim with a fiery enthusiasm.

"I think we have found something we can finally do, just you and me, Daddy. You get your pilot's certificate and we'll share wings!" said Savannah with a confidence he had never heard from her before.

"We've found our thing and it has wings," agreed Tim who could almost certainly detect the smell of burning sulfur as two Life Matches lit together.

Chapter 14: Answering the Call to Live Your Motto

Tim's office phone rang as he was trying to gather his notes for the day's managers' summit meeting. The caller ID showed it was Paul's cell phone.

"Hey, Paul, what's up? Are you ready for the big show?"

A nasal and hoarse-sounding Paul croaked, "Tim, I've got the flu and I'm really sorry, but I can't make it in today. Would you please do me a huge favor and walk the team through my presentation? You know it as well as I do and I thought you might be able to add some of your recent personal experiences as a bit of a testimonial for the content. Do you mind?"

"I'm really sorry you're sick. Don't you think we should postpone your presentation to another meeting instead?"

"We can if you're not comfortable presenting the material, but I really think that giving the cultural changes we are implementing right now, they could really benefit from hearing the Life Matches story. Yesterday, I dropped off enough Life Match books and handouts for each person to have one at the conference center. All you would need to do is share your story and present the slides. Tim, you've learned it, lived it, and now I'll ask you to lead the team into the light by sharing the spark." Paul's laugh and cough mixed convincingly on the line.

"Hey, it's not fair by using my own motto against me like that but as payment for all your support and help, I am honored to present your Life Matches story. I'll be sure to give you all the credit or blame for how it's received."

"I wouldn't have it any other way, Tim! Thank you," Paul said with noticeable relief.

Chapter 15: Fire Up! Or Fizzle Out.

When it came time for Paul's Life Matches presentation, Tim asked two of his managers to distribute the matchbooks and handouts.

"I'm taking a big risk giving you all matches to play with," began Tim. "Please, no one set off the fire alarm and refrain from lighting any of your matches. Unfortunately, Paul is home sick with the flu today, and he asked me to share this little gift with you and a story that has the potential to change your life. I know it certainly has changed mine for the better!

"If we all buy into the main points of this story, I am confident we can also successfully transform our sales organization's culture to the new team structure.

"Since you all have chosen to accept this small gift of what we will call Life Matches, would you all please place your pen in the hand that you normally write with and hold it above your heads? Now switch the pen to your other hand and sign your name using that hand on the front cover of your book...."

The next 50 minutes were a blurred mix of laughter, Tim's personal Life Matches story and Paul's primary learning points.

In closing the presentation, Tim summarized by proclaiming, "Life Matches are our personal strengths. To fire yourself up, you must first choose to accept your gifts and talents as the strengths that have been given you. Second, learn how and when to ignite your Life

Matches at the appropriate times and third, use your Life Match strengths wisely to light up the world.

"When you choose to live a fired up life and to lead others to discover their strengths through your example and coaching, you will blaze your life's trail, warm others, and become a Life Matches fire starter. By choosing these strengths-based strategies, you'll not only fire yourself up in ways that will never fizzle out, but you'll also light up our organization in ways that our competition will never be able to huff and puff out!

"I hope you will join with me in committing to do whatever it takes to fire up yourself and your teams!" concluded Tim triumphantly.

Chapter 16: Living Fired Up!

Thirteen months later and 3,500 feet higher flew Tim, a nervous Joanne, Stephanie and a confident frequent flyer named Savannah.

"How much longer until we land?" asked Joanne over the intercom from the rear seat.

"Mom, the GPS says our ETA is 13 minutes," replied co-pilot in-the-making Savannah from the front right seat where she was carefully guiding the plane under the watchful eye of a very satisfied private pilot named Tim Davis.

"Are you back there, Stephanie?" asked Tim.

"I'm right here behind you, Daddy. Hey, the trees look like broccoli!" shouted Stephanie over her headset microphone from the left back seat.

"They sure do, honey. Next stop, a week's vacation!" exclaimed Tim.

"I'm really grateful Paul gave you those Life Matches," commented Joanne earnestly.

Quickly comparing his past year's fired up life to his previous living-to-work old life, Tim agreed, "Me too, JoJo!"

As the sun was setting over the horizon and with the airport in sight, Tim thought that it was not important to worry about what if he had died that night in the hospital. For him the more important and meaningful question was, how do I choose to live this one life I've been given?

Looking down at his arrival chart, Tim noticed the now familiar square outline of his well-worn book of matches which was safely tucked inside his pants pocket.

It was a gift that he had completely accepted. Those matches had changed his life for the better and continued to serve as a friendly reminder to stay fired up or risk fizzling out.

Chapter 17: Sharing Sparks!

At the back of the book are instructions to help you make a book of your very own Life Matches.

First, you must choose to accept your unique gifts and talents as the strengths that have been freely given to only you by your Creator. You have been designed with a specific purpose in mind and your life's journey is to live out its discovery and, if you are lucky, accomplish your mission.

Second, you will have to practice in many different situations how and when to ignite your Life Matches at the appropriate times. You may receive a few minor burns to your ego in your attempts to enjoy the warmth of satisfaction that comes from living your life from your natural strengths and on purpose. Be quick to recognize and apologize to those who are closest to you who might get singed a bit while you practice.

Finally, use your Life Match strengths wisely to light up the world. You'll find that the selfish use of your Life Matches is not nearly as satisfying as using them to truly be of service to others. One of the most rewarding ways to share your flame is to invite other people into your life. Having others in close proximity to you when you are fired up may result in you sharing a spark that helps them to light one of their Life Matches. Sharing your flame is a joy that I hope you will choose to experience often!

The light of one small match can chase away an enormous amount of darkness, so imagine the world's brightness if more people fire up their strengths.

Finding activities that will allow you to combine different strengths will really set you aglow.

People will be naturally drawn to your flame when it is used properly. Your actions will certainly burn brighter than your words, so remember that someone is always watching and allow your light to lead by example.

Do not worry about burning up your Life Matches. They come with a lifetime warranty. They will last as long as you do!

I believe that one of the most wasteful choices you can make in life is to choose to not develop your strengths and to miss opportunities that may have been custom designed especially for you.

If you are ready to "Fire Up" your life, accept your free gift of your strengths and complete your Life Matches exercises. The choice is yours. Fire Up! or Fizzle Out.

Chapter 18: Steps to Firing Up!

Throughout the previous chapters, you have had a chance to learn from Tim's example. Now the hard and infinitely satisfying work of identifying your strengths and changing your thoughts and habits to begin living a more strengths-based life is yours to begin. To help you get started, do the following steps:

Step 1: Accept God's gift of your unique strengths, talents and abilities. You've been designed with a specific purpose in mind and no one else is exactly equipped for this purpose as you are.

Step 2: Sign your name using your non-writing hand on the front cover of your Life Matches book. Be sure to leave room for another signature.

Step 3: Sign your name below your first signature with your normal-writing hand. It just feels right doesn't it? You didn't decide to choose to write with one hand over the other. You were just designed with a preference. This will serve as a reminder that a sure sign of strengths is when doing something just feels natural and easy to you. When this happens take careful note, because you have just identified a Life Match in your book.

Step 4: If you need some help discovering your key strengths, you can take one of many strengths profile surveys that exist in books and online. Many online versions are free. Another good way to get some information is to review your life history up until now. Identify times when you were in your "zone" and when time seemed to slow or stop or you felt the exhilaration of being able to do something that you know you are a master at doing. Make a list of these and then also ask your friends and family to describe the things they think you are exceptionally good at doing.

Write the four key words that describe your unique strengths. These will serve as a reminder of the many more strengths that each Life Match below the words represents.

Step 5: Write a short, four or five word phrase that encapsulates the very essence of who you are. Think of this as your life's motto. Perhaps it is what you want to be remembered for, such as your epitaph. This may take some time and you certainly do not want to rush it. Feel free to use a pencil and live your motto for a while. If your motto is not working out well or if you feel called to change it, then change it. After all, you are the writer of your life's story.

There you have it: Your very own book of Life Matches to carry with you for at least the next 20 days to serve as a reminder that you are going to work hard to live your life in a way that uses your strengths and manages around your weaknesses. It will take at least that long for your new attitude to become a habit.

If you still need some help discovering what fires you up, then try the plus and minus exercise for your to-do list for a couple of weeks and you might find some clues as to what works and does not work well for you. You can also make copies of the Fires Me Up! or Fizzles Me Out worksheet and analyze each task in greater detail.

Be patient with yourself. You have a lifetime to learn how to master your Life Matches. You will find that some matches combine into unique flames you did not think of when learning how to use them individually. You will also discover that some matches are used just for a season of your life and may not call upon until a specific time. That is by design and is not something to worry about.

You will also find that you will be given some very challenging situations to test your mastery by life. Your darkest moments may be such a test. I hope you will choose to have confidence in your strengths and faith in your Creator to light your way though life's storms.

Lastly, we were not designed to live life alone. Kindle relationships with other people who are shining brightly. Together you will be able to withstand the world's huffers and puffers who will try to snuff out your flames.

I wish you success and hope that you will soon be basking in the warm glow of your Life Matches. It is called living a life on purpose that is filled with love and meaningful satisfaction.

Learn it. Live it. Share the spark!

Fire Up!

Fires You Up! or Fizzles You Out—
The choice is yours.

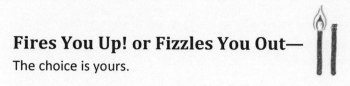

Describe how you feel when you are doing something that makes you feel "Fired Up!"

I know I am doing something that fires me up when____

_____

_____

_____

_____

List three words that best describe your feeling of being "Fired Up!"

1) _____

2) _____

3) _____

Describe how you feel when you are doing something that makes you feel "Fizzled Out."

I know I am doing something that fizzles me out when:

_____

_____

_____

_____

List three words that best describe your feeling of being "Fizzled Out."

1) _____

2) _____

3) _____

List the five activities that take up the majority of your time and energy during a typical **work day**. Rank how "Fired Up!" or "Fizzled Out" you feel while thinking about doing each activity.

	Fired Up!	Neutral	Fizzled Out

1) _____   1 2 3 4 5

2) _____   1 2 3 4 5

3) _____   1 2 3 4 5

4) _____   1 2 3 4 5

5) _____   1 2 3 4 5

List five **non-work** activities that you choose to invest the majority of your time and energy doing.

	Fired Up!	Neutral	Fizzled Out

1) _____   1 2 3 4 5

2) _____   1 2 3 4 5

3) _____   1 2 3 4 5

4) _____   1 2 3 4 5

5) _____   1 2 3 4 5

Total your scores for your five work and non-work activities that you scored above. The lower your score, the more "Fired Up!" your main activities make you feel. A score of a perfect 10 means your life is fully ablaze!

My Score: _____

Repeat this exercise with the next five work and non-work activities that take the most of your time. Keep repeating the exercise until most of your common work and non-work activities are ranked. Be sure to review a few of your daily to-do lists to find regularly occurring activities.

List three ways that you will adjust your **work life** which will allow you to invest more time and energy doing activities that fire you up!

1) _____

2) _____

3) _____

List three ways that you will adjust your **non-work** life which will allow you to invest more time and energy doing activities that fire you up!

1) _____

2) _____

3) _____

List three ways that you will adjust your **work life** which will allow you to reduce or stop investing time and energy doing activities that fizzle you out at work.

1) _____

2) _____

3) _____

List three ways that you will adjust your **non-work life** which will allow you to reduce or to stop investing time and energy doing activities that fizzle you out when you are not working.

1) _____

2) _____

3) _____

List three people who could help you to achieve working more fired up!

1) _____

2) _____

3) _____

List three people who could help you to achieve living a more fired up life outside of work.

1) _____

2) _____

3) _____

My Fired Up Life Pledge

Beginning today, I pledge to seek out ways to live my life and to do my work so that I use my God-given strengths so that   I feel "Fired Up!" I will not allow my weaknesses to hinder me from enjoying a "Fired Up!" life, by draining my energy and fizzling me out. I will discover ways to manage around my weaknesses so that they are not factors in achieving my goals and living the satisfied life that is uniquely mine. I will seek guidance through prayer and from those I love and respect to help me achieve and maintain my "Fired Up!" life. I claim the gift of my strengths and talents and pledge to use them for their highest good.

I promise to carry my Life Matches with me for at least the next 20 days as a reminder of my commitment to live a life which is truly "Fired Up!"

Signed:_____ Date:_____

Create Your Own Life Matches

Step 1: Obtain a book of 2"x2" cardboard safety matches. (Other match book sizes are fine to use but you will need to adjust the size of the label accordingly.)

Step 2: Obtain a self-adhesive, rectangular label of at least 3 ¼" x 2". Larger labels could be cut to the size of your match book. A plain piece of paper could also be used and then glued to the match book.

Step 3: Write the following on your label or paper.

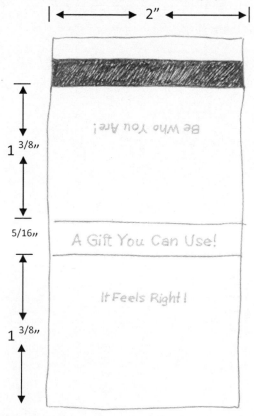

Step 4: Attach label or paper to your match book.

Step 5: Complete the Life Matches exercises and carry your Life Matches for at least the next 20 days as a reminder to live your life Fired Up!

To purchase a pre-printed book of Life Matches or for more information on Life Matches: Fire Up Your Life! visit: www.lifematchesbook.com.

About the Author

Andy has held various media and advertising sales and management positions throughout his career. He has written numerous articles for web publications and this is his first book. He holds Bachelor of Arts and Masters of Science degrees from Indiana University.

Andy resides in Indianapolis, Indiana. When not working and writing, Andy is a private pilot and a volunteer member of the Civil Air Patrol, United States Air Force Auxiliary.

Contact the author via e-mail at andy@lifematchesbook.com.